Lessons Learned
from my Cat
Laverne

Gary R. Gray

WESTBOW
PRESS®
A DIVISION OF THOMAS NELSON
& ZONDERVAN

WestBow Press books may be ordered through booksellers or by contacting:

WestBow Press
A Division of Thomas Nelson & Zondervan
1663 Liberty Drive
Bloomington, IN 47403
www.westbowpress.com
1 (866) 928-1240

ISBN: 978-1-4908-9388-4 (sc)
ISBN: 978-1-4908-9389-1 (e)

Library of Congress Control Number: 2015911035

Print information available on the last page.

WestBow Press rev. date: 07/24/2015

Contents

Contents

Acknowledgements

We are grateful to many people who helped us with Laverne and who assisted in the writing of this book.

Had it not been for the diagnostic and surgical skill of Dr. Sandra Truli Springer, VMD, Laverne would not have survived the initial stages of her illness. The Staff and Doctors and Blue Pearl Animal Hospital in Clearwater, Florida did a wonderful job of extending Laverne's life and adding to her comfort. The Staff at SEVO-Med (Southeast Veterinary Oncology and Internal Medicine) Orange Park, Florida cared for her in the last months until all treatment options had been tried. Through the last year, Dr. Michael Payne, DVM of Full Circle Animal Hospital, Callahan, Florida, who is known around town as Dr. Mike, was always available with a kind word and assistance in keeping Laverne comfortable.

As to the writing of the book, my friend Carole Barton, took an interest and offered encouragement and guidance in pursuing the project. Carole introduced me to Catherine Greenwood who edited the book. Our Pastor, Rev. Jack Varnell of Folkston United Methodist Church gave time to the project in reviewing the scriptures selected. Our longtime friends, John and Brenda Hanson read the book in its early stages and John helped select photos and edit them to see how they might look when included in the work.

Finally, Patty, deserves a great deal of credit. She spared nothing in terms of time and expense to help Laverne and keep her comfortable. Many of the photos of Laverne were taken by Patty who has a knack for catching the right moment. Patty also has a gift for proofreading and editing and contributed much to the early drafts.

To all, my deepest thanks.

Gary R. Gray

Foreword

A small gray cat peered at me from her mom Patty's arms. Laverne leaned forward and pawed in my direction as if to welcome me to her own physical exam. An unusual cat, indeed. As I ran my hands along her slender soft sides, Laverne purred loudly. The outline of a distinct lump in her abdomen formed in my mind as I felt the contours of it through her tender abdominal muscle wall. Laverne never meowed or complained. She continued to purr and stare into my eyes as if to encourage me to think good thoughts.

Rarely does a physical examination reveal a diagnosis so quickly. All I could hope was the tumor was benign, had not spread, and was fully removable. Fatefully, it was neither of the three. I gave Gary and Patty the sad news that their cat had a terrible, invasive metastatic cancer that surgery alone could not cure.

Over the months, Laverne accepted her treatments and thrived in spite of her lymphoma diagnosis. The Grays worked with a board certified veterinary oncologist for Laverne's chemotherapy and yours truly for holistic care (namely nutritional support, pain control, and Synergistic treatments to help minimize damage from chemotherapy.) Laverne lived and died well.

I applaud the Gray family's decision to treat Laverne and to be present with her until she passed naturally at home with her loved ones. We all can learn from the final days and hours of a loved one's life and should experience and cherish that time together. It was my honor to have known Laverne and you will understand as you read Gary's eulogy to his darling Laverne.

Dr. Sandra Truli Springer, VMD
Palm Harbor, Florida
February 22, 2015

Introduction

Laverne

We miss our cat Laverne.

It all started at the local animal shelter. My wife, Patty, had gone looking for a cat to adopt when a little tiger cat with a light orange belly bearing dark ocelot spots took up with her. Patty was drawn to the cat's sweet little face with the terracotta nose outlined in black. Her golden eyes were completely captivating.

Laverne, as she was called, was special— and remarkable. It wasn't just us. Everyone who met her commented on her sweet loving nature, her desire to connect with people, her grace, and her apparent appreciation for everything done for her.

We didn't know at the time that she had lymphoma and we would enjoy her company for only a little less than two years.

When the diagnosis was confirmed, we were still hopeful that she would be able to be with us for a while. As the treatment options began to diminish, I found myself reflecting on the sweet nature of this little kitty and all I was learning from her. Laverne was just being a loving cat; yet she exhibited many sterling traits that we would all do well to emulate.

As a minister of music and mental health counselor, I have assisted many people as they worked to manage relationships and losses. I couldn't help thinking of these experiences and seeing the similarities of the lessons learned as I observed Laverne.

By nature and experience, I relate life to scripture. I do not mean to elevate Laverne to sainthood, but religious references came to mind as I observed her. I hope these lessons will speak to you as they have spoken to Patty and me. Patty has many years of service as a registered nurse, and with our combined backgrounds, we chose to allow Laverne to die at home as we did our best to keep her comfortable.

If that is not your way, we understand. We each must follow our own heart as we care for our loved ones the best we can.

Choose Friends Who Will Stand By You

Patty had been going to the animal shelter on Saturdays to spend time with the cats up for adoption. She had always owned cats, enjoys the variety of their personalities, and had a soft spot for those who are less fortunate or less desirable. Originally, Patty was thinking of adopting a black cat because they are often overlooked.

One Saturday, a cat named Laverne approached Patty and did not leave. In fact, she climbed up into her lap and then onto her shoulder, setting her claws just enough to make it difficult to dislodge her from Patty's shirt.

Shelter volunteers told Patty that Laverne had been adopted before. Her adoptive family had returned her after only five months, saying they "didn't have time for her." The volunteers also informed Patty that Laverne appeared to be deaf.

"Cute name," said people who later got to know Laverne. As we would come to know, this name fit, and always elicited comments from others as Laverne was introduced. We don't know if the name was connected to the TV sitcom of the late 1970s and early 1980s titled "Laverne and Shirley" about two young women gamely making their way through life. But the name seemed to suit Laverne, and it expressed her loving, zestful, and unique personality.

Laverne was a very active and agile cat, sometimes leaping up onto a table or into someone's lap. Once on the lap, she sometimes crawled onto the person's shoulder and clung to her host while looking around from her higher vantage point. From there she enjoyed being carried around the house and outside.

Laverne investigated everything. She was not large, about the average size of a female cat. Patty loved to see the orange undercoat that was especially noticeable on Laverne's belly when she stretched out. Laverne was very alert and watchful with those golden eyes.

Since it appeared that Laverne was deaf, the shelter counseled against her adoption by a family with children, because she could be easily startled. She needed eye contact before she was approached, and she needed to be awakened gently. Those steps taken, she usually responded with a soft half meow, half purr, "meurr."

Patty phoned me from the shelter. She had found a very special cat—or perhaps the cat had found her. Could she adopt her and bring her home? Patty kept repeating that the cat had crawled up into her lap and then onto her shoulder and would not leave her alone, purring continuously. Patty couldn't believe how sweet she was. "You'll like her, Gary," she said.

I have never been an avid cat lover, though I had grown somewhat fond of our cat Tarzan, a large furry Maine Coon then more than 16 years old. I voiced my fears that Tarzan might have some difficulty adapting to another cat in the house. Patty was insistent and proceeded with the adoption.

The people at the shelter praised her for adopting an "older cat." According to the adoption form, she was eight years old. Patty was a bit surprised, as she did not see Laverne as older, but rather young, spunky, and full of life with an intriguing personality.

Once at home, Laverne cased the house, took notice of Tarzan, and enjoyed playing with various toys. She was especially fascinated by a laser pointer that her former family had left for her, chasing, jumping, and leaping to follow the little red dot, even turning somersaults in the air as she tried to catch up with it. She was very happy, active, and affectionate.

At the first veterinary appointment after adoption—a requirement of the shelter—the doctor confirmed Laverne's deafness by slamming cabinet doors and getting no response. At the second veterinary appointment, Patty asked if Laverne could really be eight years old, since she was so active. The veterinarian "re-aged her" to be three. Another opinion suggested she might be five years old–the prime of life for an active, affectionate cat.

What no one knew at the time was that Laverne had lymphoma. Patty noted to the veterinarian that Laverne seemed to consistently have loose stools. This is sometimes an indication of inflammatory bowel disease, or worse yet, lymphoma. It wasn't until we had Laverne almost a year that she made a soft cry on Christmas morning and looked rather lethargic.

We took her to our new vet, Dr. Springer, the next day. She had seen her only a week before for her first appointment. Dr. Springer took one look and said, "Kitty's in trouble."

She found a large lump in Laverne's abdomen that led to surgery. A tissue specimen was sent to the pathologist for assessment. In cats, lymphoma is incurable, as it is in people. Depending on the type of lymphoma, it may be very life limiting.

Over the course of the next eleven months Patty did everything possible for Laverne. Patty arranged her schedule and called on friends to pick up Laverne from oncology appointments when we couldn't. Patty spared no expense in making sure that Laverne had the best care, the best food, and every opportunity to have the best quality of life.

Had Laverne known somehow that Patty would stick with her no matter what?

I don't know of any way to tell, but I believe it. Animals seem to be able to sense who they can trust. Laverne chose Patty and her life was the better for it.

Sooner or later we learn that there will be times when we will have to rely on others for strength and support. We need to cultivate solid, lifelong friendships and family relationships that allow us to give and receive support. When difficult times come—and they will—we will be comforted by the relationships that offer love, support, and assistance.

It is hard for some of us to accept the concern and support of others. We want to be the strong one who helps others. Then there are others who are strong enough in their sense of self not only to accept the help of others, but to reach out when in need.

Laverne showed me the value of reaching out and connecting with others. It is important to have social supports, especially when facing difficult times. I don't know if Laverne knew this, but she lived it, choosing us to stand by her.

> **"Some friends play at friendship but a true friend sticks closer than one's nearest kin." Proverbs 18:24, NRSV.**

The Greeks have three words for love: *agape'*, *philio*, and *eros*. *Eros* is sensual physical love. *Philio* is companionship love, sometimes called brotherly love. The above Scripture in some translations refers to one who "...sticks closer than a brother" NIV. *Agape'* is unconditional love, the kind of love most people have for their children, and the kind of love God has for us. God loves us no matter what the circumstance, even when we have done something to displease God.

Our pets give us unconditional love as well as companionship. They accept us as we are, where we are, even when we are not as lovable as we could be. This may be why we treasure their company so much. We find complete acceptance in their eyes, and it seems they find a genuine joy in being with us. We don't have to *do* anything, we just have to *be* with them.

They are our friends and sometimes our defenders. I have heard many stories of cats coming to the aid of their masters to defend them against animals who have invaded the back yard. Our pets are completely devoted to us and seek nothing but our affection and acceptance. They may even lay down their lives to defend us from harm.

Such friendship is hard to find. It has been said, "No one has greater love than this, to lay down one's life for one's friends" John 15: 13, NRSV.

This kind of friendship comes at a price. We must be willing to put off our own needs and see to the needs of a friend. How often do we come home and attend to feeding our pets before our next task? When we love in this way, there is a great reward, for it becomes reciprocal.

We are too often afraid that we will be taken advantage of, or that our efforts will not be fully appreciated. Some people would say it is easier to love a pet than a human in this way, because pets are not as manipulative as humans can be. They may be right. There is, of course, the need for appropriate boundaries. Even so, can we learn how blessed it is to care for another and receive simple acceptance and appreciation?

Hang On To Those You Love. Let Them Know How Much You Care

Once Patty and I were chosen, Laverne often jumped up into our laps. When we leaned back in a recliner, she sometimes crawled up onto a shoulder and began to purr. She often slept in this position for an hour or so. This was very similar to her posture when we were standing.

Laverne seemed to enjoy being carried high on the shoulder much like an infant. She wrapped her forepaws around a shoulder and extended her claws just enough to achieve a firm hold on her host's clothing. Sometimes she placed her forepaws around the neck as if to give a hug.

This behavior of Laverne's was something that really got my attention. I have seen affectionate animals before, but not one that would seemingly "hug" their humans. To me, it was a sign of great affection, trust, and caring. It was completely endearing and one of the things that made us love her so much. Laverne was totally into us and this was her way, through physical touch, to communicate her feelings. These daily hugs revitalized the relationship. It was impossible not to stop and take it in when it was offered.

Patty often took Laverne outside in this way to look around. She maintained that Laverne enjoyed the walks and the ability to look around while feeling safe in someone's arms. Laverne would wrap her front paws around Patty as if hugging her neck or shoulder. On these occasions, Laverne would extend her chin high in the air and stretch her neck back as if to take in the fresh air and sunshine. Patty thought Laverne had a smile on her face. Laverne would watch, eyes widened, always curious and investigating as she spied passing dragonflies. At these times, Patty would stroke Laverne's little white chin, much to Laverne's delight.

Sometimes when Laverne seemed restless, Patty didn't know what Laverne wanted. But when she picked Laverne up and held her, Patty got her answer. I would say, "Sometimes she just wants to be held."

Often when Laverne would crawl up on our lap to nap with us, she would reach a paw around our side as if holding us. It was a very pleasant and comforting way to catch a short nap…for both of us.

Many studies indicate how important physical contact is in a relationship. It communicates many things, including love, concern, trust, and affection. Infants have been known to perish due to lack of touch.

It isn't enough to proclaim our love as if a single statement will suffice for all time. Relationships are as much living things as are the beings in that relationship. It is important to reaffirm our love and commitment on a regular basis through various expressions of love and affection.

This is active love—love in which we demonstrate our love and concern for each other on a regular basis. Not a day went by that Laverne didn't demonstrate her love for us in some tangible way. She hung on to us, loved us, and let us know how much she cared.

> **"Love must be sincere. Hate what is evil, cling to that which is good. Be devoted to one another in brotherly love. Honor one another above yourselves." Romans 12:9-10, NIV.**

When we lose a loved one or a pet, one of the most difficult parts of the process is learning to live without that physical touch. Touch is a tangible expression of trust, love, and connection. It makes an impression on us when our pets come to us wanting to be held or to sit on our laps. It is an expression of "brotherly" love—or perhaps we should say "companionship" love.

Can you imagine for a moment the trust involved in an eight-pound cat choosing to approach a—well, much heavier human? We could easily do great harm to the cat. Yet our pets continually risk and trust to connect with us in a physical way to demonstrate their love for us.

Now, I know some of us are huggers and others, not so much. There are other ways of expressing love and concern for each other. Physical touch is one way; kind words and acts of service are others.

The story is told of the old Scotsman who, on his wedding day, said to his wife, "Now Martha, ye know that I love thee, and we will hear no more about it."

People are not made that way. We need and should give continual expressions of love and care to those around us. Each time we have such an interaction it reaffirms our love and care, and helps nurture the relationship. This is like food for the soul and water to the garden.

Maximize Your Quality Time, Even If You Are Just Resting Together

Quality time has been defined as time we spend with others when we feel connected—not just passing time, but being in close proximity without other distractions. Sometimes we might just rest together.

Laverne demanded quality time with those in her household. If one of us wasn't available, she went to the other so she could be in that person's company. Sometimes this could be challenging if there was work to do, especially when it was computer work. Laverne created some interesting texts while walking across the keyboard.

Often we are in the same area as a loved one, but there is no real connection. To Laverne, this was unacceptable. I wondered if somehow Laverne was aware of her limited life expectancy. But then, by some degree, we *all* have limited life expectancies. We make choices moment by moment, day by day, as to how we will use our time and with whom we will share it.

I am describing an active presence—a presence in which we are aware the other person is present and we actively seek a connection. Such a connection is not possible while texting or surfing the web.

Laverne did not seem to understand that because Patty worked from home, she couldn't devote all of her time to Laverne. She would politely insist on Patty's attention by walking across her computer keyboard, or parking herself in front of the screen or in her lap, or sometimes suddenly leaping onto the desk and startling Patty. After the interruption, Laverne would accept a kindly look, or some stroking, or placement on her catnip-laced cushion in a chair nearby.

Due to Laverne's deafness, we could not call her as if she were a normal pet. Yet she was always alert to us and what we were doing. Laverne seemed to know when we were smiling at her, giving her our focused positive attention.

My counseling experience and research reminds me that the most impactful tool we have to influence our children's behavior is our positive attention. I am persuaded that our pets are affected in a similar way.

Just think of it. How often do children, pets, and others receive our direct attention only when we are displeased with them? Many learn that to be noticed, they need to misbehave. We could not scold a cat that was deaf, and she really didn't need that often. Our focused attention and a stern look was all that was required for corrective action.

We could make eye contact and hold our arms out and Laverne would come to us to be stroked, petted or picked up. She came to us readily. This simple sign language she seemed to understand. Other times, Patty could simply wave her hand in a "follow me" gesture, and Laverne would follow her all over the house. Her interest in us gave us opportunity to see Laverne as rather selfless—impressive for a cat. She rarely seemed to have her own agenda, except to be near us.

Indeed, there are times when words seem inadequate. My hospice work taught me over and over the importance of "being there." In situations that cannot be fixed, our presence communicates care and concern. Nothing we can *do* will make the situation better, but we can *be* present to show our love, support, and commitment to the relationship.

Often when touch is appropriate, our presence is *felt* by the other person. Precious are the moments in which we communicate with our loved ones in this way.

The closeness of a true friend will sustain us in difficult times. We will always remember these moments. Laverne maximized quality time even when we were "just" resting together.

> **"Do not forsake your friends and the friend of your father, and do not go to your brother's house when disaster strikes you---better a neighbor nearby than a brother far away." Proverbs 27:10, NIV.**

How many of us even know our neighbors? More to the point, how many of us have friends and neighbors with whom we feel a close connection? Do we express that connection with this kind of quality time?

During the second year of Laverne's time with us, Patty and I moved to a rural part of Florida. There when you need a hand you have to rely on a neighbor, because no one else is around. Invitations to gatherings go up and down the road by word of mouth: "Bring a dish and meet at…"

During these gatherings we spend time together talking, laughing, or just watching the fire. When someone is in need, the word goes out and people drop what they're doing to come to the person's aid. Calling 911 is good, but your neighbor will be at your side before emergency responders arrive. I think this kind of response is not possible without cultivating the friendship that sustains it. I believe that friendship is established through sharing quality time.

Yes, I think this is easier in the kind of community I describe than in a metropolitan area, where it may be easier to feel anonymous and somewhat invisible. But services are available there and agencies can respond. In cases when family members are far away, we can connect by Facebook, text, or phone, but who is there for us, present and in person?

We need to develop this kind of closeness with our friends even more in the metropolitan environment.

I have heard folks say "…a man will know how rich he is by the number of true friends he has." Developing this true friendship takes quality time. Put down the electronics and spend time together in person.

Rest Well. Sleep Trusting That You Are Safe and Your Rest Will Not Be Disturbed

Some people seem to know how to enjoy the moment—to be where they are, you might say. Cats have an affinity for this. They are seldom in a hurry. When they sleep, they find positions that indicate they are thoroughly relaxed and getting the most out of their rest.

Laverne found different quiet places to take naps. She appeared to choose them for a sense of comfort, peace, and safety. Sometimes it was in my recliner by the living room window. Other times it was on the bed or tucked between bed pillows, with only her feet sticking out between the cushions.

Laverne would curl up with her head tucked down and eyes buried in the cushion of her chosen resting place. Such a position suggested ultimate trust that she was secure. This was an especially trusting feat for a deaf cat.

Patty asked one of Laverne's veterinarians if he thought Laverne was so nice because she was deaf. He responded that deaf cats are likely the opposite—guarded and less trusting. This comment by doctor made Laverne seem all the more remarkable to us. She trusted us completely and she would go to anyone whom we trusted with her.

I marvel at how at peace Laverne was while napping. While she was sleeping, she had no ability to sense danger or the presence of another human or animal. For her it appeared easy. To me it indicated that she had complete faith in our ability to see to her safety.

In my counseling practice I have worked with many anxious people who have difficulty getting to sleep or staying asleep. They tell me that every noise, every flash of light, any indication of a possible threat causes them to feel they must always be vigilant and on guard.

I wonder if we ever fully release all of our anxieties and concerns and rest "safe and secure from all alarms," completely trusting that our resting place is safe. It seems possible with people of faith.

When we truly trust in God's watch care, we can release our worries and believe that our rest is secure, knowing that God is always watching. Apparently, Laverne felt she could rely on us to watch over her.

"He will not let your foot be moved; he who keeps you will not slumber. He who keeps Israel will neither slumber nor sleep." Psalm 121: 3-4, NRSV.

Ancient Israel always seemed to have many enemies just waiting for a chance to wipe the Israelites out. Looking at the world news today, it seems not much has changed. How does anyone find rest and sleep in such a situation?

Consider the plight of animals in the forest. The Disney classic, *The Circle of Life,* discusses the constant struggle of animals in their natural environment to "kill or be killed." We all hope mankind can come to a better solution for itself, but so far, it hasn't happened.

People of faith find their rest in God, trusting in His protection and His ultimate deliverance. The belief is that nothing can happen without God's approval and that God is watching over us and protecting us.

I believe our pets rely on us in the same way—not that I am making us into a god, though we are created in God's image and, at our best, can be like God. When our pets feel accepted and trust us, they rely on us to maintain their safety while they are resting. How peaceful they look to us, much like babies who have no fear and have complete trust in their parents to maintain a safe environment. Can we learn to trust God completely in this way?

Reach Out For What's Next.
Leave the Sorrow Behind

Yesterday is gone and tomorrow is another day. Laverne always liked to rest with one forepaw outstretched as if reaching for the next opportunity. Someone probably has done extensive research on cat brains and behavior, and probably can tell me that cats don't have a sense of past and future. That may be scientifically true. But Patty and I were impressed by Laverne's ability to let go of the past and be present, apparently anticipating good things to come.

The day after Christmas 2013, Laverne seemed increasingly listless, lethargic, and withdrawn—just not herself. Dr. Springer, our vet, determined that Laverne had developed a large tumor in her abdomen. The recommendation was to hydrate her, administer antibiotics intravenously throughout the night and, if her fever broke, to do surgery the next day. Dr. Springer advised that Laverne might not survive the weekend.

Some counseled that if Laverne was "full of cancer" it would be in her best interest not to bring her out of surgery, but to allow her to pass away while under the anesthesia.

We were not optimistic. We were devastated. We spent time with Laverne before leaving her with the vet, letting her rest on our shoulders. We thought we might be saying goodbye. Laverne just knew she didn't feel well and didn't want to be left alone. I left my T-shirt for her to sleep on.

Surgery found the tumor, which the doctor removed during a long procedure. Dr. Springer was not able to remove all of the tumor due to its close proximity to an artery. She was very concerned about Laverne even making it through the weekend. She also suspected lymphoma and sent a sample of the tissue out for testing.

Laverne healed well from the surgery and enjoyed her usual pastimes. She literally bounced back, at times having to be restrained from her usual jumping and leaping. Within days, she seemed to be feeling like her old self.

The pathology report confirmed the diagnosis of lymphoma and a very limited life expectancy. We began taking her to chemotherapy on a regular basis, and the staff at Blue Pearl in Clearwater, Florida, fell in love with her. In fact, the staff of every treatment facility Laverne visited fell in love with her. She was always cooperative and did not complain. She always took everything in stride.

When in a cage before or after treatment, she stretched out a paw as if to say, "Please take me out." Usually someone obliged. The staff enjoyed letting her sit by their computer as they typed their notes, and sometimes they carried her around on their shoulders.

More than once staff and veterinarians told us that Laverne seemed grateful for the attention and care she received. She seemed to leave any unpleasantness behind to enjoy the present. She always expected the best of others and herself. "Every day is a gift," as people say.

> **"So teach us to count our days that we may gain a wise heart." Psalm 90:12, NRSV.**

Many years ago when I was a minister of music, the children's choir at my church did a musical in which one of the songs included the following phrase: "Are you humbly grateful or grumbly hateful?" This has always stayed with me and I quote it often.

It suggests that we have a choice in how we deal with difficulties. Wise people seem to know this and practice it. They seem well aware that we have only a certain amount of time here in this world. When we spend time focused on difficulties, hurt feelings, and grudges, we lose time and have nothing to show for it. Holding on to hurts seldom changes minds or situations.

Moving forward and looking at our options can lead us to a better day. Our energies are much better spent when focused on this path. Animals seem to know this. A bright veterinarian might point out that animals have different brain structures than we do and don't remember to hold grudges like we do. Perhaps. Even so, they set a very good example for wise living.

In general, our pets are quick to forgive and move forward with an expectation that things will get better. Laverne didn't know she had a limited life expectancy, so she lived each day to the fullest. I have seen people do this when they *did* know they had a limited life expectancy. What a privilege to observe such a gift of grace!

When we live each day as best we can, looking forward, hoping for the best, and dealing with things as best we can, we enjoy life. When Paul and Silas were in prison, they prayed and sang hymns. They demonstrated that although the body may be in prison, the spirit is free. We have the ability to choose how we respond to what life gives us.

We would do well to be more "in the moment" like our pets are. They seem to accept their situation and look forward to what is next without wasting a lot of energy complaining or worrying.

Recognize That Life Is
More Than Food

Laverne was sometimes fussy about her food, as are many cats. In her case, food was critical. Good nutrition is one of the better ways to fight cancer. Patty committed a great deal of effort, time, and money into finding the best food for Laverne. Even so, Laverne sometimes rejected the food. She was always very polite. She came to her place to receive her meals and sat quite properly while waiting to be served. Sometimes she even rose up on her back paws and lifted her front paws, but never in a demanding way. It was a well-mannered request.

Laverne also could be very resourceful when she wanted a particular food. Once we heard the clamor of kitchen cabinet doors banging and were surprised to find that Laverne had managed to open the lower doors. We found her inside the cabinet vigorously tearing open the bag of one of her favorite foods. From then on, we placed a stool in front of the cabinet so she could not help herself. Later, vet techs were very surprised to hear this when we donated Laverne's extra food to them. They, too, had been impressed with Laverne as a polite, well behaved cat.

Patty's friend, Melody, often cared for our cats while we were out of town. She said Laverne leapt up onto the counter, almost overshooting the mark, and waited patiently as her food was prepared. Perhaps this was as much about companionship as it was about the meal. Laverne wasn't rushing for the food dish as much as she was spending time with Melody while she prepared the meal. People often seem to gather in the kitchen to spend time with one another as a meal is being prepared, so perhaps Laverne was being sociable, too.

Laverne also seemed to eat more when we were with her than when we weren't. It was as if she wanted company while she enjoyed her meal. Research indicates that we also will eat more when we are in the company of others than if eating alone.

When she was served something that didn't seem right to her, she would paw at the floor and quietly leave it behind.

We have had other cats who would eat anything and demand more. Not Laverne. This puzzled me. I wonder if, when we are in tune with what our bodies need, we seek that which will truly sustain us.

Even so, for all creatures, there comes a time when food is no longer of interest. Patty wanted to continue to nourish Laverne, but Laverne knew it was of no more value. Quietly, politely, she rejected food as she began to spend a great deal of time in bed. She did desire that the bed be in an area near our activity, and if left alone for a time, Laverne would use all of her strength to seek us out.

We got the message, and we were careful to keep her near us as long as that seemed to be important to her.

> **"Therefore I tell you, do not worry about your life, what you will eat or what you will drink, or about your body, what you will wear. Is not life more than food, and the body more than clothing." Matthew 6:25, NRSV.**

It appears that some of us live to eat. We are preoccupied with our next meal. Yes, food and nutrition are important. But Laverne reminded me that there are more important things, such as our relationships. They are nourished and strengthened through respectful interactions, such as politely waiting, helping with meal preparation, or sharing time over a meal.

The Scripture also reminds us that life is about much more than food or clothing, yet we spend much time and effort in acquiring these items. In my part of the country, clothing is pretty simple—pocket tees and blue jeans. Here more time is spent on courtesy and friendship than on the acquisition of things. A cook-out is not so much about the food that is prepared as it is the time spent sharing in fellowship.

In the end, it is not our body that will survive, but our spirit. When we develop a loving, respectful spirit, we develop something that will last into eternity. I am not sure Laverne knew this, but how marvelous that she could remind us of this lesson!

Refresh With Flowing Waters

Laverne had a peculiar way of getting a drink. She did not much care for drinking water out of a bowl. She preferred to drink from water flowing out of the faucet over the sink. I know some other cats do this, too. It seems like a great expenditure of energy to leap up onto a kitchen counter and balance on a sink just to drink water from the faucet.

I wondered if Laverne had been a stray at one time and had learned to drink from a flowing stream to get fresh water that wouldn't harm her.

Once she had positioned herself, she would patiently and quietly wait for one of us to turn on the faucet so she could drink her fill.

She was as smart as she was polite, and she did not want to inconvenience anyone. I wonder if, given enough time to study the mechanics of it all, she might have figured out how to turn on the water for herself. After all, she had figured out how to open the cabinet doors.

She was always very careful not to knock anything over or upset anything. She loved to wait on the counter by the kitchen door for us to return home so she could greet us. From this vantage point, she could look through the windows in the kitchen door and look out into the garage. Once she spied us, a soft chorus of meows would be silenced only by being taken up in someone's arms.

Her preference for flowing water was puzzling. She even preferred it to bottled water—and our tap water is not very tasty. To Laverne, flowing water was the way to get fresh water. People who spend time in the woods and have had survival training know that flowing water is usually clean water. To take in flowing water is to refresh the body and re-hydrate without risking illness.

I can't help being reminded of the life properties of "living" water flowing for us. We can go several days without food, but we won't last more than a day or two without water. Flowing waters has been a metaphor for the life-giving properties of the Spirit.

> **"...he will satisfy your needs in a sun-scorched land and will strengthen your frame. You will be like a well-watered garden, like a spring whose waters never fail." Isaiah 58:11, NIV.**

Many scriptures refer to "flowing waters." These are often used as a metaphor for the Holy Spirit, who refreshes and restores. Sitting beside a body of water, especially a flowing steam or a waterfall, is a well-documented way of relaxing and cleansing our mental state. It seems to restore one's spirit.

Are animals somehow closer to God than people are? I think they are just more "in the moment" and "in tune" with their Creator, who reveals to them what is good. I have met many wise souls and excellent woodsmen who have mastered this ability. They are able to be still and hear all that is around them, and be led to that which is good for them. I believe our Creator will do this for us as well—when we listen.

Investigate Your Surroundings Thoroughly

Dr. Springer was the first to say about Laverne, "She investigates everything." Perhaps because of Laverne's hearing deficit she was very careful to know everything about her surroundings. Whether she was at a medical office or in our home, she checked out everything. Yes, cats are generally curious, but it was something more with Laverne. She was always careful and always respectful, but she was thorough in her investigation.

Laverne didn't get into mischief and she wasn't destructive. She just wanted to carefully and completely examine her surroundings, and she did so with the same well-mannered, loving spirit that she did everything else.

I marveled at Laverne's commitment to living life as normally as possible with her hearing deficit. We learned that some cats develop deafness as a result of illness or infection. Perhaps she had been deaf since birth and really didn't know she had a disability. I believe she was a curious cat who balanced her curiosity with thorough investigation.

I wonder if it gave her a sense of comfort and safety to know where things were and what they were. Then again, she seemed to enjoy checking out new items. Laverne was completely and fully present wherever she was. Her investigations included people as well as her surroundings.

I know of no instance when she did not willingly go to a stranger to drape herself over a shoulder. She seemed always to trust Patty's judgment in this regard. This often occurred at the office of a veterinarian, where Laverne would trustingly go to a stranger, amazing everyone gathered there—strangers and technicians alike. The beneficiaries of such encounters seemed to count themselves fortunate to be the recipient of such affection.

Maybe this was all part of Laverne's nature, but what a great way to do life—to be fully aware and fully present in all of our surroundings *and* with all the people with whom we come into contact. It was as if each new person who entered her life was a fascinating new friend to greet, explore, and engage.

I have admired several great and notable people who seemed to have the gift of presence—to be fully present and engaged with everyone they encountered. They have the ability to make you feel as though they have no place to be other than with you, that there is nothing more important in all the world than spending time with you in that moment—no checking the watch or the new text on the cell phone.

How would our relationships be different if we were able to be more curious, more interested in everything and everyone that life has to offer? How much richer would life be for us, and those with whom we interact, if we could be fully present with each other?

> **"Keep alert, stand firm in your faith, be courageous and be strong. Let all that you do be done in love." 1 Corinthians 16:13-14, NRSV.**

So how did Laverne remind me to "stand firm in the faith?" I can't say that Laverne had a faith in the sense that people do. However, if she had a statement of faith, I believe it would have sounded much like the words Paul shared with the Corinthians in his first letter to them. They had many issues going on, many of which people have today. It would have been easy for them to get into difficulty.

Paul exhorted them to be watchful, to keep alert to all the things that could cause a missed step, to be strong in their faith, to be who they were called to be, and at the same time, to be trusting in the "spirit of love." Laverne was the embodiment of the spirit of love while being alert and engaged with everyone and everything she encountered.

Express Appreciation For Kindness. Be Humbly Grateful For Everything Done For You

Laverne probably had more visits to the veterinarian in two years than most cats do in a lifetime. One would think that this would grow old and wear thin after a while. Laverne seemed to accept the providers as friends and trust that they were there to help her. The doctors and technicians commented on how Laverne actually seemed grateful and appreciative of any efforts or interventions to help her.

She displayed this even when the intervention seemed a bit painful or uncomfortable. She seemed to understand that everything done for her was intended to give her comfort and a better quality of life. Laverne would *show* her gratitude with a gentle look, a soft head rub, a hug, or a little lick.

My theory, which comes from observation of other animals, is that when an animal does not have an easy life in the beginning, the animal seems truly to appreciate kindness later on. I believe Laverne may have started out on the street with little food, water, shelter, or comfort. Sometimes this has a different effect on humans. Animals seem more likely to accept any kindness or provisions offered them. I also believe that animals are able to sense our intentions and know whom they can trust.

Of course, there are situations in which abused animals can become mean and aggressive. People can be that way, as well. Even so, it seems that Laverne *chose* to gratefully accept the attention and intervention, even when unpleasant or painful, trusting that they were meant to help her.

As Laverne "hung out" with veterinary staff, sitting beside the computer as they typed their notes, her posture and demeanor just seemed to say, "Thank you for all you are doing to help me. Do you mind if I spend some time with you?" In the same way, she would invite herself out of her cage, as if she were aware of her gift of presence and the joy it gave to others. Laverne wanted to share her gift of presence in appreciation for their gift to her.

Laverne had found the secret to being content, which is to accept the situation, knowing that some situations are better than others, and all will pass in time. To complain or display disapproval only diverts energy away from dealing with what is at hand. When you assume, as she did, that everyone you encounter wants the best for you, you can appreciate their efforts and be thankful for their service.

> **"Those who love with a pure heart and are gracious in speech will have the king as a friend." Proverbs 22:11, NRSV.**

Laverne made friends wherever she went. People were drawn to her. Her face invited others to connect with her, but it was much more than her good looks. She had a spirit about her, and although she did not speak to people as we would, she definitely communicated with them. Somehow, she communicated a message of love, friendship, and acceptance.

When it came to those providing care for her, it seemed to go further. She somehow communicated her appreciation for their efforts on her behalf. The outcome was to win over every doctor and technician with whom she had contact. They all became her friends and commented on her attitude of acceptance and how she expressed her thanks. It was almost magical to watch how those relationships evolved. Those people now tell us how much they miss her visits.

I wonder how our relationships might be transformed if we could relate to each other in this way? Proverbs suggests that having this kind of attitude and spirit allows us to enjoy the friendship of those in high positions. In the time of Proverbs, no one was more important than the king, so if you made a friend of the king, you had some special quality or winsomeness about you. You were also assured of favorable, if not royal treatment.

If we would love others in this way, with a pure heart and gracious speech, how different our relationships would be! To treat one another with the grace and respect afforded to royalty would change the dynamic of the relationship and facilitate mutual appreciation and affection for one another.

Some years ago, I encountered a man who offered rental properties to people in difficult circumstances. He always referred to them as "Saint Mike" or "Saint Joe," depending on their names. I had a strange, special feeling in my conversations with him. I had never been addressed as "Saint Gary," but I immediately felt special and respected. Our conversation was one of the most cordial I can remember, as if I were doing him a favor by talking to him.

In my days as a hospice counselor, I visited people who had a special respect—almost a reverence—for others, always giving thanks for any act of service or kindness. I always went away feeling as though I should thank them for allowing me to spend time with them. Indeed, I often ended our conversations with, "Thank you for allowing me to spend some time with you." When you think of it, their time was very precious, as it would seem to be much more limited than mine.

To approach each other graciously and gratefully, expressing our appreciation for one another, would surely have a significant impact on our interactions and relationships.

10

Suffer With Grace. Be Present To All Who Bring Love and Meaning To Your Life

This lesson, for me, is the most vivid. I can hardly remember a time when Laverne hissed at anyone or became defensive when receiving care or treatment. Once when she was sitting on the kitchen counter on that Christmas day before her surgery, she gave a soft, pleading cry. She must have been uncomfortable from the large tumor lurking in her abdomen.

Laverne sometimes greeted us with a meow, but in general, she was a quiet cat. Patty remembered bringing her home from the shelter—a 30-minute trip—wondering about her, as Laverne didn't make a sound. Laverne wanted to be near us all the time. When she didn't feel well, she lay down on a bed or a chair, and eventually took to her own small bed.

Through every examination, every treatment, every pill she had to swallow, she never fought us or complained. Rather, she seemed to understand and accept that these interventions were necessary to her health and well-being.

Most of the time, she continued her best efforts to be a present and loving companion, interested in us and in what we were doing. At times, this made it hard for us to know when she wasn't feeling well. Patty developed a knack for discerning the very subtle signs, and she sought treatment for Laverne immediately to help alleviate her discomfort.

To me, this most remarkable lesson is the ability or *choice* to continue to focus on our relationships rather than on our personal difficulties. We often greet one another with, "How are you?" Yet I am not sure we ever really want to know, and if someone begins to tell us, we often look for an escape.

How we treasure people who can overlook their difficulties to engage us with enthusiasm and genuine interest! These are special people and animals who overlook their own discomfort to be fully present with us, enjoying the moment and our company. To suffer with grace is to continue to be engaging, loving, and involved with those whom you love, even through your discomfort.

"I know what it is to have little, and I know what it is to have plenty. In any

and all circumstances I have learned the secret of being well-fed and of going hungry, of having plenty and being in need." Philippians.4:12, NRSV.

In this Scripture, Paul thanks the people in the Philippian church for their concern and gifts to him. At the same time, he illustrates that when people have found peace and contentment, the things of this world do not matter. Good times and bad times come and go; it is our relationships that are important. These relationships will transcend our time on earth.

This steadfast, accepting spirit gives us strength to deal with any difficulties. For Paul and those of the faith, verse 13 tells the secret: "I can do all things through Him who strengthens me" NRSV.

Now, I don't believe animals have the ability to accept Christ. But somehow, many of them seem to be imbued with a special spirit of acceptance to be able to deal with whatever comes their way. Indeed, they can demonstrate the spirit that Paul described.

Laverne did that. Not only did she suffer with grace, but she was able to communicate her appreciation of any intervention to ease her suffering. For her, it was all about relationship and spending time with her friends. To choose to focus in this way avoids wasting precious moments in self-pity, and allows us to bask in the warmth of time spent with special friends.

In Closing

Laverne was not doing well. On Tuesday, November 25, 2014, Patty took her to the oncologist. The doctor could do nothing further. We had been hopeful that if the tumor shrank enough, Laverne could benefit from radiation, but it was not to be.

It was a very difficult day. We knew it would come, and the finality of it was overwhelming. I had to leave work early, as I could not function well enough to do my job.

That afternoon I built a little pine box for Laverne so we could bury her in the backyard, which she loved to visit while riding on Patty's shoulder. The next day I went to the local hardware store, bought some stick-on black letters, and spelled out her name across the top of the box. If someone found it one day, he might be alerted that the contents were special.

Some people might wonder why I would go to all this effort for a cat. People who have enjoyed a special relationship with any non-human creature will know. We wanted to honor Laverne's memory and the love we shared. The building of the box was hard and tears flowed. It seemed to be part of the healing process. Even now, it is difficult to tell this part of the story with any sense of composure.

Patty and I had decided to keep Laverne at home until the end, because she did not seem to be in pain, and we had some medications to help comfort her. She loved being near us. We wanted to continue to give her every opportunity to be in our company, and we wanted to be with her, too. Some may choose another path for their pet. People must do as their hearts lead.

Laverne became more lethargic on Thanksgiving Day, spending more time in her bed. She had always been a very tidy cat, and she was fastidious to the end, using her last bit of energy to drag herself to the litter box.

Friday afternoon when Patty gave her the pain pill, Laverne seemed startled. I believe she was starting to slip away from us. Early the next morning Patty came to me and said, "She's gone." I went into the walk-in closet where we had Laverne's bed, and she lay lifeless in her bed on her favorite blanket.

Laverne died in the early morning hours on Saturday, November 29, 2014.

It was a frosty morning. When the sun came up, we dug a hole in a corner of the backyard. We then gathered her up in that favorite brown and pink blanket with the little cat paws, and placed her in the box with a note:

LAVERNE

If you are reading this then you have found the remains of our dear cat, Laverne. We have left her this way as she was very special to us. She was one who loved being around people. She loved to be held and to rest on our shoulder. She was gentle, loving, and patient. We had her only two years, the last year trying to give her the best quality of life possible as she fought lymphoma. She died 11/29/2014.

Please allow her remains to continue to rest undisturbed.

Gary and Patricia Gray

We felt some peace afterward knowing that Laverne was at rest. As the days progressed, her absence in the house was noticeable. She had been a vibrant and loving presence, a true friend.

We are reminded again and again of our loss, and we feel sad.

I have spent my professional life as a minister and counselor. I have walked the path of grief with many families who have lost loved ones, both human and otherwise. I am more convinced than ever that each loss is different. Grief is expressed and worked through in different ways. The kind and quality of the relationship has significant impact on our grieving.

For many people, the loss of a beloved pet is a loss in which they regret that the time was so short, that the pet died before living a full life. I will not compare this to the loss of a child, as some do. In Laverne's case, she was in the prime of her life, and it seems we were cheated out of many years of a mutually loving relationship.

45

Often when a pet or other loved one has lived a long and full life and has become infirm, the end seems to make sense, even though it may still be very difficult. We wish our loved one could return to full health and enjoyment of life; yet, we see the suffering. We can come to a place where we are ready to let someone go rather than see the suffering continue.

Reconciling a loss is a process. It is not a straight path. There are days when Patty and I think we are making progress, and there are days when it seems that life will never be the same. There are many ways to help the grieving process: talking with others, writing about the loss, reviewing pictures. At times, the memories are very painful. Yet, the events that created the memories are what made the relationship meaningful in the first place.

A hospice client said, "It is all about learning to remember with a smile instead of a tear."

These memories—these "pictures" in our hearts—can never be taken from us. At some point, we can come to see that it is a good thing to remember.

Relationships impact us, test us, and teach us. May we be open to the lessons that come with each relationship and hold them close beyond the loss.

I felt very sad that such a loving cat was taken so early in her life. Such unconditional, trusting love is not easily found.

Patty and I treasure our time with Laverne. We hope these thoughts and lessons learned will help you live fuller, more completely in relationship with others, whether they are human or otherwise. Take every opportunity to express your love and affection to those you love. You will find it blesses you and them.

Rest well, Laverne. You lived well. You taught me well. Rest well, little love.

Printed in the United States
By Bookmasters